Enjoying Toddlerhood

Quick Tips for Busy Parents

Heather E. Trem

Enjoying Toddlerhood: Quick Tips for Busy Parents

EnjoyingToddlerhood@yahoo.com

To my husband, Joe, who always provides me with
continuous support no matter what I do.

To my children, Taryn, Brady, and Lyla,
who taught me more than they will ever know.

To my friends who encouraged me to write this book.

Thanks!!

CONTENTS

"Parents are often so busy with the physical rearing
of children that they miss the glory of parenthood,
just as the grandeur of the trees is lost when raking leaves."

~ Marcelene Cox

Introduction

This book is intentionally brief. I cut right to the chase because I know that the parent of a toddler has precious little time for reading, even if that reading is about toddlers. This book will take some of the guesswork out of caring for your toddler. I address the topics that I have found are the most often discussed in my social circle like potty training, binkys, and discipline.

Trying to parent a toddler and deal with everything else going on in your life without losing your cool can present a huge challenge. Remember, you are not alone. Every parent has felt like you have at one point or another. Since I have been there, done that, tried this, tried that, my hope is to bring you some relief with my tips so that you can enjoy toddlerhood!

CHAPTER 1

POTTY TRAINING

"Every accomplishment starts with the decision to try."

Anonymous

Y OUR TODDLER IS MOST likely going to be wary of a giant bowl of water that actually eats pee pee and poo poo, but once he shows an interest in it, jump on that opportunity! For example, if he tells you he went in his diaper, or insists on being changed immediately, or wakes up from a nap dry, or asks about your experience while you are going to the bathroom (come on, you can't pee alone, right?), it's an opportunity that you shouldn't waste.

When you hear the words "potty training," your first instinct may be to cringe, but with the right attitude and a few tips that I'm going to share with you, potty training can be accomplished in one weekend (no, really!). I'm the mother of Irish twins—children born within twelve months of each other—so admittedly, it was easier for me to potty train my son because he wanted to be just like his older sister. But whether it's your first child that you have to potty train or your last, the goal is the same: make it seem to your child that going on the potty is the most wonderful thing in the world!

Your toddler's potty training experience depends as much on you as it does on him. For the busy parent, the hardest part about potty training is committing to it. Once you start potty training, you need to be patient, stay positive, be consistent, and follow through with it—anything less will just confuse your toddler and draw out the process unnecessarily. That said, if you begin potty training and you find that your child is going in his underwear more often than in the toilet, you may want to wait awhile and aim for another weekend to try again.

You can set the stage for a positive potty training experience for your toddler by taking him to the store to pick out his own underwear. This little bit of independence makes him feel like he is a big boy, with such an important job as choosing his own Lightning McQueen undies! Also, if he does have an accident while wearing them, you can say something like, "Oh, Lightning is so sad that you went pee pee all over him." When I said that to my son, he apologized to his underwear, and he told me that next time he will go on the potty! Since he chose the underwear himself, he was able to identify with it more.

I also recommend using a potty chart. The potty chart does not have to be fancy—a piece of construction paper with your child's name and "Potty Chart" written at the top is fine. Buy some stickers that you know he'll love, and every time he uses the toilet, let him pick out his own sticker to place on the potty chart. Again, he feels some independence and control by picking out his own sticker. Stock up on a few presents from a "dollar store" and explain that if he earns a certain number of stickers—five stickers and then ten and then twenty, etc.—he will get a present. Children just love the fact that they are rewarded (don't we all!).

With potty training, the more practice and positive reinforcement the better. So to encourage the process, hydrate your child with juice boxes, water bottles, popsicles, etc. The key to potty training is for your child to go every hour on the hour for two days straight while wearing underwear. Even if he doesn't actually go, at least he is sitting on the toilet and getting used to it. Don't let him sit for more than five minutes because two things may happen—he will become bored or agitated—and neither one is a positive feeling to have while potty training. Expect a few accidents, and when they occur, be supportive—just encourage him to use the potty next time. You don't want him to feel like he disappointed you because then he may lose interest altogether. You'll be surprised at how smoothly potty training can go if you are committed, patient, and positive!

CHAPTER 2

PICKY EATERS

"Dear God, I pray for patience and I want it right now!"

∼ Oren Arnold

I F YOU WANT TO enjoy toddlerhood, you need to choose your battles. This is the shortest chapter for one reason: you can't force a toddler eat something when she doesn't want to! Don't get upset because she eats the same food all the time—chicken nuggets, macaroni and cheese, and hot dogs are the staple of my toddlers' diets—you may get bored with it, but your toddler won't! This really used to upset me, but then I thought, "Why? Who cares?" She likes knowing what to expect—there are no surprises in taste when she recognizes the meal—and it makes it easier for me to plan meals and grocery shop, since I can plan on preparing the same meal at least twice a week!

I'm not saying don't try to introduce your toddler to new foods. I'm saying that if you take the this-is-what-we're-having-and-too-bad-there-are-no-other-choices approach, chances are you will lose that battle. If you tell—tell, don't ask—your toddler to try one bite of something new, you'll usually get a positive response. Also, try giving her a choice between two meals. She'll feel like she has a say in the matter, and she just may surprise you by choosing the one that you didn't think she would try!

Who doesn't like a good PB&J sandwich?! I couldn't believe it at first, but the answer is my toddlers (I know, shocking, right?)—they're just not big fans of bread. So instead of stressing all of us out, I got creative. I used cookie cutters to transform sandwiches into dinosaurs and other fun shapes that at least got them to try it, which is a huge breakthrough for toddlers!

Focus on the fact that your toddler is eating and is healthy. It truly doesn't matter if she repeatedly eats the same meals now because in time and with a little patience, understanding, and creativity on your part, her tastes will change. As long as you can sneak in some fruits and vegetables (try serving them first, with nothing else on the table) then you can't ask for anything more. So relax and enjoy your toddler!

CHAPTER 3

Binkys

"The best thing to hold onto in life is each other."

∾ Audrey Hepburn

E VERY PARENT KNOWS THAT the importance of a binky to a toddler cannot be overstated; however, getting your toddler to give up their binky does not have to be traumatic for your child (or for you). The key phrase is *give up their binky* as opposed to *you take away their binky*. As I've discussed throughout this book, providing appropriate opportunities for your toddler to feel a little independence and in control of things that are important to them goes a long way.

Frankly, I don't think a child over three should have a binky. I only allowed my toddlers to have a binky at naptime and bedtime—they didn't walk around with them while they were awake. For some parents, especially if it's their last baby, they don't care how long their child has a binky because no one ever sees a kindergartner with one, right? While that may be true, the longer your toddler has a binky—or paci or whatever cute little name you have for it—the worse it may be for their teeth and the harder it may be for them (and for you) to give up their binky.

Once you've decided it's time for your toddler to give up their binky, there are many fun, interesting ways to do this. Get creative! I've heard of the binky fairy where at bedtime the child places their binky in an envelope, basket, or box—something special that you decorate just for the occasion—and in the morning, the child wakes to find that the binky fairy has taken the binky and left a small toy in its place and perhaps a note.

When the time came for my daughter to give up her binky, I gave her two months' notice, so she wouldn't be taken by surprise when the time came. I told her that during her third birthday party, she will say bye bye to her binky, and she just assumed that the rule was that three-year-olds can't have binkys! So at her birthday party, I tied her binky to a balloon and gave it to her. Then everyone went outside and counted down from ten, and when we reached one, she let go of her binky-balloon and the whole party waved bye bye to her binky. We told stories about how the birds use the binkys for their babies (I know, not great for the environment, but it worked well).

Even though my daughter willingly let her binky-balloon go at the party, I thought that we would still have a rough couple of nights. But guess what? It was only one, and it wasn't that bad! She whimpered a little bit but then went straight to sleep when we told her that in the morning, she would have to check to see if the birds had left her a big-girl toy because they were so happy with her for sharing—and to her delight, they did!

CHAPTER 4

Routines

"A child wants some kind of undisrupted routine or rhythm.
He seems to want a predictable, orderly world."

∽ Abraham Maslow

I'VE DISCOVERED THAT TODDLERS love routines. Just like they like to eat the same foods because they know what to expect when they taste it, they thrive on knowing what to expect throughout the day. Establishing a routine is not only comforting to your toddler, it benefits you too. Knowing that the day is planned will make you instantly more relaxed and calm (as calm as the parent of a toddler can be). As I'm sure you're aware, but it bears repeating, your child picks up on your energy. So the calm energy that a routine affords you is much more preferable for your toddler than the nervous energy of a parent who is scattered and rushing throughout the day.

You can start establishing your routine by telling your toddler three basic things: lunchtime, naptime, and playtime. This way they are prepared (and it is not a shock) when you happily announce, for example, that it's time for a nap! I love to tell my toddlers about the day for two reasons: they learn how to tell time, roughly, and they learn patience. For example, if I say to them, "We will go to the park after naptime," they get a vague understanding that "after naptime" means in the afternoon. Also, the questions about if it's time to go yet (which are not annoying at all) are cut dramatically if I say "after naptime" instead of "not now," which also allows us to focus on our present activity.

I also make it a point to show them the clock. They always look at the kitchen clock while we are eating. Our lunch is around 11:00 every day, so I got in the habit of saying it's 11:00, even if just to myself, and they have caught on. I haven't taught them the half hour yet; although, I always say the correct time if they ask, so they hear that it isn't always an exact o'clock. After dinner, if they ask for snacks ahead of time, and I say, "No, it isn't 7:00 yet," they accept this and wait patiently. Sometimes they'll just run into the kitchen to see if it is 7:00! They've also learned to eat a little more at dinner, especially if I remind them no snacks until 7:00!

Once you have a routine established, it is refreshing to watch it play out. My kids brush their teeth before breakfast, and then right after eating, they race to their rooms to get dressed. They are comfortable in their environment.

They understand that naptime comes after lunch—so on good days, they will run in there ready to rest, and the rest of the time there is less arguing because it's the way they know and they expect it.

On the flip side, I'm not saying that you shouldn't mix it up every so often either. Toddlers also need to know that sometimes a day is different from others. If something unexpected happens, act like it is a special treat that they get to do something or go somewhere. Field trip! Be prepared if they call your bluff, though. I really wanted my kids to stay up later when we had family coming over and we were waiting for someone, but they were intent on keeping their routine: it was bedtime and they were tired—so good night. That was fine too though! Doesn't it drive you crazy that even if they do stay up past their bedtime, they still wake up on schedule the next morning? You'd think that they would sleep in a little later the following morning, but no, same time every day. Ahh, routines...

CHAPTER 5

Staying Busy

"A child reminds us that playtime is an essential part of our daily routine."

Anonymous

I F THERE IS ONE thing I've learned while raising my toddlers, it's the need to stay busy. I'm not talking about your routine—the busy-all-the-time stuff that is part of everyday life—I'm talking about doing something, getting out, breaking up your day, week, and month! Incorporating fun activities into your routine and anything you can mark the calendar with that says "special day!" are the fun kind of busy that toddlers love.

Since I'm a teacher, it's natural for me to base my schedule like a classroom where each day of the week has a theme. For example, Monday is library day. Check your library for story hour or just go and pick out some books and then read a couple to your kids while you're there—they may listen more attentively in a different environment.

Tuesday is "gym" day. Any day the weather is nice, I take them outside to play in the yard or we go to a park. If there aren't any parks around you, head to the nearest elementary school—there should be a nice playground there. Where I live, we don't see too many nice days for outside fun, so I take them to an indoor inflatables arena to let them jump around. Anything that gets everyone up and moving and having fun sounds like a good activity for gym day to me!

Wednesday is art day. If there is a holiday or birthday approaching, use it as inspiration for art projects. I use Google a lot to get toddler craft ideas. Another idea is to work on one letter a week and make art projects that start with that letter and even have snacks that start with it too. For example, while working on the letter "A," incorporate the "A" theme into your day: have a snack that starts with that letter; have your child bring you a toy or anything in the house that starts with that letter; and have an art project that is focused around that letter. I'm not much of an artist, so I Google the picture (airplane) and have the kids color it. You can add your own flair to it! Cut it out and glue it to blue paper, and then glue on cotton balls for clouds. Teach them to glue first; they don't understand how it works unless you say "turn it over, then press!" Older toddlers/preschool age can try to cut out their own pictures with safety scissors if the picture isn't too detailed. Incorporating themes works too: like under the sea, teddy bears, and zoo animals. Then your toddlers can learn while doing a fun project! Make sure you hang the art project up and change it every time you change letters because they love to see their work displayed!

Thursday is cooking day. Sometimes we actually get out bowls, spoons, and ingredients, but most of the time, it's something super easy like making cookies with store-bought cookie dough. The kids have fun putting it on the tray: they like the texture, and they like to nibble a little on the dough (I know, I hear my mom yelling at me about worms!). Setting the oven timer helps them to understand what "in a few minutes" means, and smelling the cookies baking but having to wait until the timer goes off helps them with patience as well. We also like to enjoy our "creations" with friends, so we invite them to our house or we bring our goodies to their houses. It's a win-win situation: the kids are excited to share the treats we made with their friends and then play for a while too, and I get the chance to hang out with another adult, which is wonderful even if only for a short while.

Friday is toy day. I'm sure you were surprised at how quickly toys took over your house; I know I was. Even though I made it a point to donate toys that were rarely played with, it seemed as though toys had taken my house hostage! So I gathered up half of the toys and put them in a closed container in the basement. Then every Friday, I "rotate" a few toys. The kids get excited upon seeing a "new" toy to play with! Also, it gives me a chance to wash the stored toys before bringing them out. Sometimes, I give my kids a wipe and let them clean the large toys. For some reason, they love this!! To a toddler, a computer is just as much fun as a physical toy. So on Fridays—okay, sometimes we go on the computer for a little every day but winters are long!!—I set the timer for five minutes for my daughter, and when it goes off, five for my son. Aside from what they learn on educational-but-fun websites, they are also practicing patience and sharing, and they even help each other as they each have a turn playing. We love starfall.com, PBSkids.org, and of course, playhousedisney.com.

I believe it is important to have something to look forward to every month—both for the kids and for the parent. An outing to McDonald's PlayPlace, Chuck E. Cheese, the zoo, or even the toy store is special to a toddler. If there is a birthday, holiday, or special event coming up, I write it on the calendar with a bright marker. My helper (the kids take turns) tapes up the date—you can find the numbers 1-31 at a dollar store or make your own on cut-out squares—and then together we count down how many more days until the event. Singing the *Days of the Week* song will help them understand the concept of days and numbers together. You can sing it to *The Addams Family* theme song.

> "There's Sunday and there's Monday, there's Tuesday and there's Wednesday, there's Thursday and there's Friday, and then there's Saturday. Days of the week (clap clap), days of the week (clap clap), days of the week, days of the week, days of the week (clap clap)."

Equally important on the calendar is a day for the parent. Something special for you to look forward to once a month. A mani-pedi, lunch or dinner with friends, heck even a trip to the mall by yourself will do. You don't have to go anywhere fancy, but you do need a day to look forward to too! Time that is 100 percent yours is healthy and rejuvenating—it is not selfish—and it makes you a better parent. Knowing you have a certain day once a month helps to get you through the days that may seem a little too long!

CHAPTER 6

Discipline

"Discipline doesn't break a child's spirit half as often as the lack of it breaks a parent's heart."

Anonymous

ALTHOUGH THE TITLE OF this book is *Enjoying Toddlerhood,* this chapter on discipline could easily be in a book titled *Enjoying Parenthood.* The time and effort you spend disciplining your toddler is the difference between a calm home and a chaotic home possibly for the next two decades!

When your child became a toddler, you didn't just let him have the run of the house, you put barriers between him and potential harm—baby gates, outlet covers, etc.—you established physical boundaries for his well-being. Childproofing a home is neither convenient nor quick, but you did it because you love your child more than you could ever have imagined possible. You need to approach disciplining your toddler from the same perspective: just as childproofing your house establishes physical boundaries, disciplining your toddler establishes behavioral boundaries for his well-being.

Disciplining their toddler is not something any parent looks forward to, but if you start early with the right attitude and a properly executed, consistently applied timeout technique, your child will have no other frame of reference—he will know with 100 percent certainty what to expect if he chooses not to listen to you. You, the parent, are the boss! It's your job to teach your child right from wrong, acceptable versus unacceptable behavior, and respect for himself and for others. The longer you wait to discipline your child, the harder it will be for everyone when you do. I believe that you teach people how to treat you, and if you allow your toddler to disrespect you, your other children, or your home, you have essentially handed over your power to a toddler. Good luck getting it back.

I cannot overstate this: discipline must be practiced as early as possible. Once your child understands you, it's time to start. When you give your toddler a command, he has to know you are serious. He will absorb the tone of your voice and realize that you sound a little different, and he'd better listen! Unless of course, you make the mistake of adding "okay" to the end of a command. "Sit in timeout, okay?" Tagging "okay" onto the end of a command negates the importance of what you have said, and it turns a command into a request, and your child will think that he has a choice in whether to obey you or not. Simply ending the command puts to rest any ideas he may have had about you changing your mind!

When your child does something that he understands he is not supposed to, get down to his level, look him in the eyes, and in a calm, firm voice say no. As he gets older, explain why you are saying no. For example, if your child hits his sister, try saying, "Using your hands to hurt your sister makes her cry. Hands are for eating and clapping." At this point, if you just say no and move on, it's an invitation for him to try again later.

If the behavior persists, place him in timeout. A good rule of thumb for the amount of time in a timeout is one minute per year of age. Choose a place for timeouts that is away from the action where there is nothing fun or entertaining to do. Placing him in his bedroom where he can play defeats the purpose of a timeout! I use the bottom step; some people use a chair or stool in a hallway, even sitting on the floor is fine. Once you have designated a place for timeouts, it's important to use it consistently.

Your demeanor while you are disciplining your child is important. You need to communicate a calm resolve to your child with your tone of voice and through your body language. A good mental clue for yourself or verbal clue to your spouse is the phrase "respond don't react." Thinking this to yourself or saying it aloud to your spouse may help you or your spouse to ignore the instinct to raise your voice and to calm down instead. If you want to fly off the handle because you are so angry, another good technique is to count to ten; if that doesn't do it, count as high as you need to so that you can respond calmly instead of reacting emotionally. The physical act of placing your child in a timeout is not always pretty—it can literally mean "placing" him on the chair—but it should never be hurtful. If he runs into another room, calmly go and get him.

Once he is in the timeout area, get down to his level, look him in the eyes, and calmly but firmly explain why he is there. Your explanation should connect his actions with this consequence and make it clear that it's his behavior that is unacceptable, not that he is "bad." Do not say things like "that's bad," or especially, "you're bad." This is a very impressionable time, and telling your child that he is "bad" is one of the most hurtful things you can say to a toddler. An appropriate explanation is something along the lines of "You're sitting on the step because you used your hands and hurt your sister after Mommy told you not to. It is not acceptable for you to hurt your sister. You didn't make a good choice, so you have to sit here until Mommy comes back to get you." Then get up and walk away. Do not respond to anything that he says to you as you leave.

If your child stays in the timeout area until you return great! If he doesn't, understand that he is testing your resolve. So if your child leaves the timeout area before the timeout is over, calmly go and get him, place him back in the timeout area, and restart the clock on the timeout. Do not say anything or respond to anything that he says to you. Be prepared to do this for as long as it takes for him to stay in the timeout area for the full timeout. If it takes an hour, it takes an hour; if it takes two hours, it takes two hours; how ever long it takes, once you begin a timeout, you must see it through to the end. If you do not follow through with a proper timeout now, you will teach him that he doesn't have to listen to you because you have just demonstrated that you don't mean what you say and there are no consequences for inappropriate behavior or for disrespecting you.

Once your child has completed the full timeout, go over to him, get down to his level, look him in the eyes, and tell him again why he is in the timeout and that he needs to apologize for his behavior. "Mommy put you in a timeout because you used your hands to hurt your sister after Mommy told you not to. You need to apologize to your sister for hurting her and to Mommy for doing something I told you not to do." After he apologizes, give him a hug and a kiss, and then move on.

To sum up, when disciplining your toddler, remember to respond calmly instead of reacting emotionally, get down to his level and look him in the eyes, explain why, and follow through. Keep in mind that it's the behavior that's bad, not him, and encourage good choices.

About the Author

HEATHER E. TREM is a high school gymnastics coach and a substitute teacher. *Enjoying Toddlerhood: Quick Tips for Busy Parents* is her first book, and all of the tips and techniques that she writes about come from her experience working in the toddler room at a daycare center, classes she took while earning her teaching license, and the most rewarding and demanding experience of all: being the mother of three, two of whom were Irish twins (children born within twelve months of each other). Since Heather's first two children were born eleven months apart, she had to learn and learn quickly!

Heather lives in Willowick, Ohio with her husband, Joe, and their three children: Taryn, Brady, and Lyla. She loves to read books, and she has written several children's books (so far for her children only). Heather takes the time to play with her children every day making sure that she fully enjoys their toddlerhood because she knows that it will be over all too soon.